THEN & NOW

LEWISTON

Opposite: The *c.* 1908 landscape of the Lewiston Village, from Seneca Street south of the Presbyterian church and cemetery, has dramatically changed over a century. On Center Street from Fourth Street east to Fifth Street resided H. Fraser, International Brewing Company, G. B. Carter, W. Carter, M. L. Raymond, Frontier House, O. E. Fleming, and A. Burne. (Courtesy of the Historical Association of Lewiston.)

THEN & NOW

LEWISTON

Suzanne Simon Dietz
Amy Lynn Freiermuth

For my high school sweetheart Raymond

—Suzanne

For my buddy Neal and baby girl Matti

—Amy

Copyright © 2010 by Suzanne Simon Dietz and Amy Lynn Freiermuth
ISBN 978-0-7385-7312-0

Library of Congress Control Number: 2009942516

Published by Arcadia Publishing
Charleston SC, Chicago IL, Portsmouth NH, San Francisco CA

Printed in the United States of America

For all general information contact Arcadia Publishing at:
Telephone 843-853-2070
Fax 843-853-0044
E-mail sales@arcadiapublishing.com
For customer service and orders:
Toll-Free 1-888-313-2665

Visit us on the Internet at www.arcadiapublishing.com

ON THE FRONT COVER: Joshua Fairbanks and Benjamin and James Barton built the Frontier House in 1824. The "Finest Hotel west of Albany" served Gov. DeWitt Clinton, James Fenimore Cooper, Charles Dickens, Edward Prince of Wales, Jenny Lind, and Pres. William McKinley. The hotel was the Mason's transfer stop in 1826 for the abducted William Morgan, who threatened to divulge Masonic secrets. The development of the closed Frontier House has been at the heart of a legal battle. (Courtesy of the Historical Association of Lewiston.)

ON THE BACK COVER: This automobile was headed west on Center Street just beyond the Frontier House on the right. Traveling east, Center Street becomes Ridge Road, one of the oldest and most traveled Niagara County roads along the ancient Lake Iroquois, predecessor to Lake Ontario. Efforts are underway to resurrect the tracks and early-20th-century trolley service from Niagara Falls to Lewiston. (Courtesy of the Niagara Falls Library Local History Department.)

CONTENTS

ACKNOWLEDGMENTS

We are deeply grateful for the contributions of the following individuals and organizations in our effort to document the changes of Lewiston throughout its rich history. In alphabetical order: Sister Rosemary Anthony, osf; Barnabite Fathers; Rachel Baron; Diane Bayger; Eric Beecher; Martha Williams Bennett; Kevin Beutel; Susan Beyer; Andrea Blakelock; Mary Boatman; Josh Bodie; Patrick Bradley; Carol Brandon; Michael Broderick; Harry T. "Hap" Brown; Paul Calkins; Fred Caso; Lynn Wolfgang Catalano; Betty J. Clark; Chris Clay; Judy Cline; Terry Collesano; Maureen Fennie Collura; Bob Darin; Michele DeLuca; Leo DiBello; Gary Di Camillo; Michael Di Camillo; Daniel DiLandro; Anthony DiMino; Michael A. Drahms; Terry Duffy; Anne Dykstra; Douglas J. Etue, Linda Feldman; Diane Finkbeiner; Gregory Fletcher; Harold "Neal" Freiermuth; Judy Freiermuth; Donna Garfinkel; Michael Gillis; Randy Gorzka; Darwin A. Haseley; Peggy Hatfield; Pamela Hauth; Bryan Held, Tim Henderson; Elizabeth S. Jordan; Maureen Kellick; Margaret Lacki; Eleanor Larson; Eric Madia; Joyce Malinchock and Greg; Diane Maroon; Tim Marren; Eric Matthews; Dominic Notarianni; Linus Ormsby; Louis Paonessa; Paul Pasquarello; Father Sebastian Pierro; Lori Presti; Bryan Printup; Pastor Walter Printup; Rich Pysz; Carmelo Raimondi; Linda Reinumagi; Carole Schroeder; William Scully; Sister Mary Serbaki, osf; Gerianne Simon Serchia; Emery Simon; Lee Simonson; Buddy Smallwood; Tammy Snelgrove; Cici Soluri; Sister Margaret Sullivan, osf; Gerald Treichler; Louise Wasko; Anne Welch; Francis Williams; Victoria Wolcott; Matt Winterhalter; Jerry Wolfgang; David Young; and also the Brickyard Brew Pub and BBQ; Eddie's Art Shoppe; E. H. Butler Library of Buffalo State SUNY; Historical Association of Lewiston; Jane's Cafe Express; Lewiston Family Dental; Mount St. Mary's Hospital; New York State Office of Parks, Recreation, and Historic Preservation; New York State Power Authority; Niagara Falls Library Local History Department; Niagara Frontier Bible Church; *Niagara Gazette*; Niagara University; Pekin Fire Company; Sanborn Area Historical Society; Sisters of St. Francis; Tuscarora Environment Office; Upper Mountain Fire Company; Valery Contracting, Inc.; and Waste Technology Services.

We are very thankful to our spouses, Raymond Dietz and Neal Freiermuth, who helped review the text and photographs and for their support of this historical journey. We also appreciate Nannette Simon (one of Suzanne's nine sisters) and Julie Siegel (Amy's friend) for copyediting. And we enjoyed three-year-old Mattilynn Freiermuth's company while she patiently accompanied us as we walked the streets, climbed hills, and explored historic Lewiston sites for research and photo shoots. All modern images are courtesy of photographer Amy Lynn Freiermuth unless otherwise noted.

INTRODUCTION

The Town of Lewiston was formed from the Town of Cambria by an act of the New York State Legislature on February 27, 1818. Following the formation of Erie County, the current borders of Niagara County were established and the Village of Lewiston was designated the temporary county seat from 1821 to 1823. Former president Jimmy Carter described the Village of Lewiston, incorporated on April 17, 1822, as "the most historic square mile in America." The sovereign Tuscarora Nation, Model City (Model Town), Sanborn, part of Pekin, and the early hamlet of Dickersonville (known as Hardscrabble before the War of 1812) are situated within the town.

New York State governor Morgan Lewis was the namesake for Lewiston, originally called Lewis Town. Lewis fought in the American Revolution, commanded the American forces at the Battle of Fort George on May 1813, and later was appointed commander of Upstate New York. Daniel Tompkins defeated Lewis in the 1807 election. Tompkins played an important role in reorganizing the state militia and used his personal property as collateral for loans to finance the War of 1812 in New York. Francis Lewis, father of Morgan Lewis, was one of the signers of the Declaration of Independence.

Lewiston was the birthplace of the thundering cascades of Niagara Falls more than 12,000 years ago. As the falls eroded more than 7 miles, Lewiston's history helped to shape the expansion of our country. The portage or "carrying place" from Lewiston around the falls was key to the development of the Great Lakes area and settlement of the West. Frenchman Chabert de Joncaire constructed a trading post in 1719, establishing the first permanent structure built by a white man in Lewiston. John Montresor built the earliest recorded railway, an inclined tramway up the escarpment, in 1764.

On December 19, 1813, the British crossed the Niagara River at Five Mile Meadows and burned Lewiston. Other significant periods of Lewiston's history were the Great Overland Route and stagecoaches to the east, the old Military Road and cattle drives to supply Old Fort Niagara, one of the final stops of the Underground Railroad and freedom for slaves, the Great Gorge Route via the electric railway, the magnificent steamships bringing thousands of visitors from Canada, and the Robert Moses Power Project.

The Earl W. Brydges Artpark opened in 1974 and has become Western New York's premier destination for outdoor concerts and theater productions, which brought more than 400,000 tourists and local patrons in 2008 to the village. Adding to this revival and transformation of Lewiston are the Whirlpool Jet Boat tours, considered one of the top five adventure rides in North America; the Niagara Power Vista's view of the power facilities in the United States and Canada; events such as the Smelt Festival in May, the Christmas Walk, and Tour of Homes; the Castellani Art Museum with more than 3,700 works of art dating from the 1870s to the present; the wine tours along the escarpment; and much more through the ongoing sponsorship and efforts of Artpark and Company, the Historical Association of Lewiston, the Lewiston Council on the Arts, the Lower Niagara River Region Chamber of Commerce, community service organizations, and support of local government officials.

Lewiston has begun preparations for the binational 1,000-day commemoration of the War of 1812, which will bring national and international attention as tourists visit the historic sites of the battles on the Niagara Frontier and in Lewiston, and celebrate the 200th anniversary of peace with Canada.

CHAPTER 1

THE WAR OF 1812

The United States of America under Pres. James Madison declared war on the British and their colonies on June 18, 1812. American general George McClure's order to torch Newark (Niagara-on-the-Lake) and earlier burning at York (Toronto) eventually brought British forces, seeking revenge, to Lewiston. Lewiston and Queenston's rebuilding efforts following the war are visible in this early 1900s image. (Courtesy of William Scully.)

On October 13, 1812, an assault force of several hundred men from the New York militia left the Lewiston Landing and began rowing across the Niagara River to invade the British colony of Upper Canada. A historic plaque about the invasion is on the boulder at the present park. The Nelson Cornell Hotel (1897–1927) in the image below was the third hotel since the 1840s built and burned at the landing site. (Courtesy of William Scully.)

Capt. John Ellis Wool and his troops scaled the Queenston Heights. The Redan Battery was overwhelmed, and the British retreated. Shortly after, Major Sheaffe, with fresh troops, outflanked the Americans and Lt. Col. Winfield Scott surrendered. The British victory was tempered by the loss of Maj. Gen. Isaac Brock. The Lewiston-Queenston Bridge in this photograph from the 1930s was replaced in 1963 by the new bridge built upriver. (Courtesy of the Niagara Falls Library Local History Department.)

At dawn on December 19, 1813, Maj. Gen. Phineas Riall, with about 500 regulars and Native American allies, crossed the Niagara River, landing at Five Mile Meadows, and descended on the village. The Americans were unable to stop the raid and burning of Barton's mansion, several stores, warehouses, and other homes. The Niagara Peace Memorial at the meadows below Stella Niagara was completed in May 1965 and features four panels, including Pres. John F. Kennedy's image. (Courtesy of Sisters of St. Francis.)

An earlier home of Maj. Benjamin Barton was burned during the War of 1812. Troops were camped on the bluff area. Cannons on the west lawn faced Queenston. Barton was quartermaster of General Porter's brigade of volunteers. After the war, he rebuilt the beautiful mansion shown in this early-20th-century photograph. In 2005, the extensively renovated Finkbeiner home was open to the public for the Historical Association of Lewiston's popular annual Tour of Homes. (Courtesy of Diane Finkbeiner.)

In 1928, a Niagara Falls Historical Society plaque at the Niagara Falls Country Club marked the midway point between two trenches used by the American forces during the War of 1812 in defense of the Niagara River border and Fort Gray, "located on the Niagara escarpment about 300 yards to the north." The club made history in 2009. For the second time, an entire round of the Porter Cup was scratched due to rain. (Courtesy of the Historical Association of Lewiston.)

The remains of Maj. Benjamin Barton and Captain Nelson, soldiers from the War of 1812 and also original settlers, were buried in the old village cemetery adjacent to the First Presbyterian Church. In 1830, the cornerstone for the church was purchased, and in 1964, there were several additions. A recent cemetery restoration project was undertaken by the Lewiston Council on the Arts and the Historical Association of Lewiston. (Courtesy of the Niagara Falls Library Local History Department.)

The pre-1906 postcard identified the building at 476 Center Street as a "relic of the War of 1812." The identification "little yellow house" was recorded in the county clerk's office as early as the 1850s. The village purchased the former law offices of John Simon, who practiced in Lewiston for almost half a century. Cathy and Jonathan Boas, proprietors of the Little Yellow Chocolate House since January 31, 2008, delight village goers with truffles and chocolate goodies. (Courtesy of William Scully.)

Marquis de Lafayette spent the night here in 1825 with Tuscarora chief Nicholas Cusick. Peter Porter wrote that during the War of 1812, "3 miles away (from Lewiston) the friendly Tuscarora Indians, on their reservation, gathered to protect (the fleeing citizens) and drove back the pursuing British Indians," while "constantly blowing on cow horns." The 1820s Kelsey's Tavern was used for medical offices in 1972. The expanded building is the office for Coldwell Banker Talarico. (Courtesy of the Historical Association of Lewiston.)

The Lewiston Museum opened in 1973 in this former church built in 1835. The museum was rededicated November 23, 2009, after an 18-month closure for substantial renovation and the addition of permanent exhibits documenting the French explorers in 1720, the War of 1812, the Underground Railroad, and Lewiston's heyday steamship era. Above, from left to right are Pamela Hauth, Lee Simonson, and Michael Broderick. They are members of the Historical Association of Lewiston that is dedicated to preserving history. (Courtesy of the Historical Association of Lewiston.)

CHAPTER 2

HOUSES OF WORSHIP

The Dickersonville Methodist Church cost $2,020 when the church was built in 1853 on land donated by Rev. Sheldon Townsend. The Townshend Acts bore the name of Sheldon's ancestor Charles Townshend who spearheaded the legislation, which helped spark the American Revolution. The church, photographed by John Kudla in 1980, is now a private home. (Courtesy of the *Niagara Gazette*.)

In 1954, a group of Barnabite priests began Our Lady of Fatima Shrine in a field on Swann Road. St. Anthony Mary Zaccaria founded the Clerics Regular of St. Paul, commonly called Barnabites, in Milan, Italy, during the 16th century. The Dome Basilica was constructed in 1963. The 24-foot sgraffito peace mural behind the altar was recently relocated to the sacristy area as part of the extensive expansion and remodeling. (Courtesy of the Barnabite Fathers.)

The new granite exterior for the ambulatory surrounds the entrance to the basilica. The top of the dome provides an angel's view of the spectacular 15-acre Christmas light display from Thanksgiving to January 6 each year. More than 130 life-size marble and bronze statues represent saints from all races and walks of life. The National Basilica to Our Lady draws tens of thousands of pilgrims each year for prayer and renewal. (Courtesy of the Barnabite Fathers.)

Rev. Elkanah Holmes of the New York Missionary Society preached the Baptist doctrine interpreted by Nicholas Cusick to the Tuscaroras in 1800. The Baptist faith continued amidst the interruptions of the War of 1812, migration to Kansas of many members in 1846, and fires in early church buildings. The church in this early 1900s image burned in 1974 and was replaced by the brick structure. The sesquicentennial of the Articles of Faith was celebrated February 2010. (Courtesy of the Tuscarora Environment Office.)

Niagara Frontier Bible Church formed in 1969 as an independent Bible church. The original 12 charter members purchased the former St. John's Lutheran Church in Youngstown. A decade later, the growing congregation bought DeChantal Hall in Lewiston. The next move was in 2003 to the Lutheran Church of the Escarpment on the corner of Bronson Drive and Upper Mountain Road. The roofline was reshaped and a larger sanctuary was added, adjoining the original building. (Courtesy of the Niagara Frontier Bible Church.)

On September 14, 1953, Rev. Leo Smith, Diocese of Buffalo Auxiliary Bishop, dedicated Hennepin Hall, a former restaurant, and the home of Judge Sherburne Piper in 1833. Piper taught at the Lewiston Academy and was known as the "Hanging Judge." The Sisters of St. Francis of Penance and Christian Charity taught the students and resided in the hall, now the rectory for St. Peter's Church, built in 1970 to accommodate the growing congregation. (Courtesy of the Niagara Falls Library Local History Department.)

Construction of the manse was completed in 1875 by the First Presbyterian Church Society at 605 Center Street and has been extensively remodeled since the 1970s era photograph. Rev. Samuel Plant, substitute minister for Pastor Jeremiah Odell from 1870 to 1881, was the first to live in the manse. Rev. Charles LaPlaca was the last minister to reside here. The building was sold for a private residence in 2003 to Bruce and Jackie Sutherland. (Courtesy of the Historical Association of Lewiston.)

The chapel of Our Lady of the Sacred Heart was built at Stella Niagara in 1908 in traditional Gothic design. Since the 1922 image, significant renovations inaugurated in 1964 by Mother M. Isabelle Reilly included the design and production of religious icons including the curved sgraffito altar screen by artists Joseph Slawinski and Michael Baranowski. Recent changes in the body of the chapel were to facilitate the needs of the Sisters in the Health Center. (Courtesy of Sisters of St. Francis.)

L. C. Williams photographed the original Mount St. Mary's Hospital Chapel on the sixth floor in March 1965. During 1971, the chapel was moved to the first floor, the emergency room expanded, and a new ambulance entrance was added. On November 14, 2003, a blessing was given for the new Imaging Center and Women's Image Suite. The St. Francis Guild staffs the hospital gift store, and under Pres. Gerianne Simon Serchia raised $65,000 in 2009 for the hospital. (Courtesy *Niagara Gazette*.)

St. Peter's Church was built in 1908 from Hotchkiss' quarry stone and converted to a theater used by Artpark in the 1990s. Owned by Steve Washuta LLC, the building became a temporary home for the 2009–2010 season of Niagara University theater. Rachel Baron, Leo DiBello, Eric Madia, and Victoria Wolcott were on stage during a dress rehearsal of *The Dearest of Friends and Other Plays* by Horton Foote directed by Amanda Lytle Sharpe and Maureen Anne Porter. (Courtesy private collection.)

CHAPTER 3

INSTITUTIONS OF LEARNING AND HEALTH

Stella Niagara opened their 2008 centennial year celebration with the Marble Orchard production *Star of Niagara* in collaboration with the Lewiston Council on the Arts. Robert F. Kennedy Jr. challenged 1,000 guests to enhance the Franciscan value of respect for the earth. The top left field, in Frank Seed's 1940s photograph, became a town park. (Courtesy of Sisters of St. Francis.)

Ground was broken for the seven-story Mount St. Mary's Hospital in August 1962 to replace the Sixth Street facility. Patients were moved into the new hospital on November 14, 1965. Sisters of the Third Order of St. Francis started the original hospital in 1907 and in 1997 turned over sponsorship to the Daughters of Charity. Today Mount St. Mary's Hospital and Health Center continues to care for the sick and the poor. (Courtesy Niagara Falls Public Library Local History Department.)

INSTITUTIONS OF LEARNING AND HEALTH

The statue of the Blessed Virgin Mary in front of the first Mount St. Mary's Hospital, known as "House on the Corner" in this 1912 photograph, at Sixth Street in the Falls was moved to the front of Our Lady of Peace Nursing Care Residence. The inscription on the statue's plaque was inscribed, "presented by Rev. A. A. Bachmann." The 250-bed facility opened in 2003 and provides long-term, skilled, and rehabilitative care. (Courtesy of the Niagara Falls Library Local History Department.)

The class of 1952 was the final group to complete their education at the Red Brick School that now houses the Village of Lewiston Offices. The village celebrated its 150th year in 1972 with Mayor John W. Fermoile and trustees Richard Webb, J. Richard Moses, Harry Dixon, and George Clark. The Lewiston Police moved from the Red Brick to their new offices at the Lewiston-Porter Central School in 2009. (Courtesy of the Historical Association of Lewiston.)

The prestigious Lewiston Academy opened in 1825 at Ninth and Center Streets and drew students from Canada and the United States. The academy was supported by the profits of the Lewiston ferry to Canada and closed when the building of the bridge to Queenston ended ferry operations, resulting in a lack of funds to maintain the school. The building was torn down in the 1930s and has been replaced by Academy Park. (Courtesy of the Historical Association of Lewiston.)

Vincentian tradition is the hallmark of Niagara University. The campus was purchased in 1856. Clet Hall was the first building erected in 1862, shown in this late-19th-century image. Our Lady of Angels Seminary was the forerunner of the university. Laboure Hall, one of Clet's two wings, is home to the Leary Theatre, under renovation with plans for reopening April 2010 with the final season production of Cole Porter's *Anything Goes*. (Courtesy of the Niagara Falls Library Local History Department.)

INSTITUTIONS OF LEARNING AND HEALTH

From 1909 to 1939, the three-story convent at Niagara University provided a residence for 24 Little Sisters of the Holy Family brought from Sherbrooke, Canada, by Father Walsh to care for the dining halls, kitchen, and laundry. The Bernadine Sisters of St. Francis followed from 1939 to 1947. The Colleges of Business Administration and Education occupy the 56,000-square-foot academic complex, and Bisgrove Hall was added in 2007 to the former Perboyre Hall. (Courtesy of the Niagara Falls Library Local History Department.)

The trailers between the first senior high school, now South Elementary, and the junior high, photographed in 1971, provided additional classrooms for the influx of students that began with the construction of the Power Project. The Lewiston-Porter Central School formed July 1, 1947. Classes were first held at the Creek Road campus in September 1952. The present high school, out of view, opened in 1970. Extensive renovations at the district also altered parking areas and entrances in 2009. (Courtesy Eleanor Larson.)

INSTITUTIONS OF LEARNING AND HEALTH

The Sisters of the Sacred Heart of Jesus purchased the former board and administrative offices building of the Lewiston-Porter Central School in 1974 for Sacred Heart Villa, a private elementary school for pre-K through fifth grades. An addition was built for living quarters for the Sisters, the congregation's national headquarters, and novitiate. The Sisters have educated more than 3,000 students and continue their half-century of service to the community. (Courtesy of the Historical Association of Lewiston.)

Msgr. P. J. Tronolone, Rev. Edwin Cuddihy, and Rev. Raymond Russell participated in the groundbreaking for St. Peter's Roman Catholic School in the fall of 1957. The $160,700 two-story building opened with six classrooms; four were added later. In 1971, principal Sister Julie O'Stroske began an innovative reading program using cassette tapes for grades one and two. Energy conservation resulted in extensive remodeling of the building facade in 2003. (Courtesy private collection.)

INSTITUTIONS OF LEARNING AND HEALTH

The Tuscarora School for primary grades, in the foreground, was located at the corner of Mount Hope and Walmore Road and moved in 1954 for a residential home. A smaller schoolhouse for the younger students, living quarters for the principal, and a clinic were behind this building. Construction began for the new brick school in 1952. Today the school educates pre-K to sixth grades and also houses the Tuscarora Nation's medical and dental clinics. (Courtesy Tuscarora Environment Office.)

The Stella Niagara parlor "reception room" in the 1930s eventually was converted into two foreign language classrooms. In 1963, the elementary, cadet program, and high school enrolled a total of about 300 students, the largest parochial enrollment in Niagara County at that time. The mission of Stella Niagara Education Park is to instill the Franciscan heritage in an academic atmosphere. The Middle States accredited school provides a Montessori program and kindergarten through eighth grades. (Courtesy of Sisters of St. Francis.)

INSTITUTIONS OF LEARNING AND HEALTH

CHAPTER 4

LAKE ONTARIO
ORDNANCE WORKS

An appeal for patriotism in January 1942 for the construction of a TNT plant began an environmental legacy that continues to haunt the Lewiston and Porter communities. The site, pictured in this 1980 photograph, was chosen because of its proximity to chemical manufacturing plants, Fort Niagara, electrical power and water, and the New York Central Railroad. (Courtesy *Niagara Gazette*.)

Tugwell and Wiseman Canning Factory, on the west side of Model City Road, employed 300 workers during the peak season of 1934. The annual payroll was about $90,000. The company contracted with farmers to grow 500 acres of peas and 500 acres of tomatoes as well as other vegetables, which were packed at the plant. In 1942, ordnance construction headquarters functioned in the canning factory. The headquarters of Modern Corporation has been operating a non-hazardous solid waste facility since 1964. (Courtesy of the Historical Association of Lewiston.)

Percy Morgan, Lewiston town supervisor, urged property owners in Model City on January 7, 1942, to cooperate with the court order for almost immediate possession by the government of the homes and farmlands within the arsenal site of approximately 7,500 acres. The property owners were not paid for six months and obligated for 1942 property taxes and mortgage interest. Most homes were burned, a few were moved, and others near the boundary seen in this current photograph remained. (Courtesy *Niagara Gazette*.)

Earlier in this Lewiston Town Highway building on Model City Road, Niagara County Farm Bureau's agricultural defense committee set up an information office with the cooperation of a number of organizations including the Federal Land Bank Association to assist the dispossessed residents. Lewiston attorney J. Boardman Scovell represented 34 property owners who unsuccessfully questioned the government statements relative to amounts paid and the lack of assurance of future payments. The building was razed in 2007. (Courtesy of the Historical Association of Lewiston.)

Mickey Osterreicher photographed the 166-foot concrete silo at the Lake Ontario Ordnance Works, which contained 2 pounds of radium and 10,982 pounds of uranium oxide. Joseph P. Kirchue, site supervisor, holds a 1965 inventory of other materials stored at the compound in this January 1979 photograph. The silo was dismantled and is no longer visible from Porter Center Road looking west, but the half-life of the buried materials is more than 100,000 years. (Courtesy Buffalo State College Courier-Express Collection.)

The Niagara Falls Storage Site, 191 acres on Pletcher Road, holds radioactive residues from the production of atomic bombs that destroyed Hiroshima and Nagasaki and materials K-65, R-10, L-30, and L-50. The white-suited technicians with Geiger counters are gone, but what remains here and at CWM Chemical Services, LLC, a hazardous waste facility, concerns citizens and the Residents for Responsible Government. The Department of Environmental Conservation (DEC) draft of the Hazardous Waste Siting Plan has been the focus of public information sessions. (Courtesy *Niagara Gazette*.)

CHAPTER 5

BEYOND THE VILLAGE

The "spoils area" acquired by the New York State Power Authority in the 1950s became the dump site for thousands of tons of excavated rock from the construction of the Power Project. The late 1960s brought public concerns over reputed chemical dumping under the rock by some Niagara Falls area plants. (Courtesy New York Power Authority and Historical Association of Lewiston.)

The tunnel for the Lewiston branch of the New York Central and Hudson River Railroad ran under Center Street parallel to Eighth Street, presently the Colonial Valley Plaza. Along the line at Eighth and Cayuga Streets was J. W. H. Kelly Coal Yard. Following the line north, the freight house operated on the west and the cold storage on the east between Cayuga and Center Streets. At Oneida Street, the line headed east to Model City. (Courtesy of the Historical Association of Lewiston.)

An estimated 13 million passengers enjoyed the Great Gorge Route, which began in 1895 and closed in 1935 after a severe rock slide. The ecological change that followed over the next 70 years began with grasses, forbs, and shrubs from seeds dispersed by nature and wildlife. Ideal natural conditions set the stage for pioneer tree species and eventually forest species, explained Michael Drahms, New York State Office of Parks, Recreation, and Historic Preservation and photographer of the present trail. (Courtesy Niagara Region New York State Parks.)

In the early 1900s, the Niagara Gorge Railroad tracks ran north, almost parallel with Lower River Road, in the town through the fruit farms. Orin Dunlap took the photograph. From the carbarn on Water Street, the line ran north to Onondaga, looped south on First Street, then east to Center Street, and north to Fifth Street. The horses from the Grainge ranch, the former Hopkins fruit farm, use the railroad path today. (Courtesy of the Niagara Falls Library Local History Department.)

#I Lewiston & Youngstown Frontier RR.

The railroad connecting Lewiston to Youngstown was dedicated on July 21, 1898. Lewiston and Youngstown Frontier Railway's engine was stopped at the Youngstown Cold Storage between the cooling tower and icehouse. A northbound train left Lewiston at 8:00 a.m., Stella Niagara at 8:07 a.m., Youngstown at 8:20 a.m., Fort Niagara at 8:23 a.m., and arrived at Fort Niagara Beach at 8:35 a.m. On several days of the week, 11 trains left northbound through Lewiston. The storage closed in 1996. (Courtesy private collection.)

Lewiston Hill was described as in a "dangerous state" during 1917 discussions for improvements. The road descended the hill at a steep angle and made two sharp turns through a railroad viaduct. In 1961, the Niagara County Board of Supervisors urged work on the $3.5-million project to begin as soon as possible, calling Lewiston Hill a "hazard to motorists." The project straightened the road and made the slope more gradual. (Courtesy of the Historical Association of Lewiston.)

Trees and extensive remodeling of homes on Mountain View Drive since the 1930s have obscured the spectacular view from the road of Brock's Monument and the Niagara River. This is now the home of Francis and Marie Shenk Williams. Harris and Mary Williams, Francis's parents, moved their family next door on the right 60 years earlier. Martha Williams Bennett climbed cherry trees as a girl by the Daggett's home at Lewiston Hill. (Courtesy of the Niagara Falls Library Local History Department.)

An overlook on the Canadian side of the river near the Adam Beck Station was created in 1959 for a view of the American Robert Moses Power Project construction, which eventually employed more than 11,000 workers and produced 2.19 million kilowatts of electrical energy. In 1961, Pres. John F. Kennedy called the project an "outstanding engineering achievement" and "example to the world of North American efficiency and determination." (Courtesy New York State Power Authority and Niagara Falls Library Local History Department.)

In 1958, the power authority photographed the productive Patterson family farm on the western boundary of the Tuscarora Nation. John and Caroline Mt. Pleasant owned the farm at one time. Caroline was known as Jikonsaseh, an important political figure for the Haudenosaunee Confederacy in the late 1800s. The filling of the reservoir with a perimeter of approximately 7.2 miles, covered the farm, 29 other Tuscarora households, and also forced the rerouting of two major creeks, sources of fish for many Tuscarora families. (Courtesy Tuscarora Environment Office.)

Hudson Brothers Milling Company, open for 54 years on Niagara Street in Sanborn, produced Daisy Pastry Flour, acclaimed locally as the finest pastry flour on the market in 1936. Calkins purchased the A. L. Syposs and Son feed mill in the 1990s and replaced it with the lumber warehouse. Paul Calkins, third generation of D. F. Calkins Lumber, grew up unloading railroad cars for his grandfather's lumber business, which began in 1928 adjacent to this building. (Courtesy Sanborn Historical Society.)

Royal T. LeVan, of LeVan Hardware Store, called to order the first meeting in 1926 of the Western New York LeVan Pioneer Association. The LeVan family, French Hugenots persecuted for their faith in Picardy, came to America in 1727. LeVan was a member of the Sanborn Fire Company. Girl Scout troops and other community organizations ran fund-raisers in the store during the 1940s. Today antiques are sold at the Sanborn Old General Store. (Courtesy Sanborn Area Historical Society.)

The Pekin Volunteer Fire Company was organized in 1932 on Upper Mountain Road. William Strassburg was the first president, and Fred Wethey was the first fire chief. In 1936, the company was one of the first in Niagara County with a water tank truck. The old firehouse stood until 1985. From left to right are Kevin Beutel, Darwin Haseley, Tammy Snelgrove, Douglas Etue, and Bryan Held. Members of the fire company serve Lewiston for $1 a year. (Courtesy Pekin Fire Company.)

BEYOND THE VILLAGE

The Upper Mountain Fire Company formed in 1959 to safeguard homes in the escarpment due to the State Power Authority project, which accelerated growth in the area. The reservoir location impacted accessibility of fire protection from the Lewiston Fire Company No. 2 at Colonial Village. William Latham of the SPA negotiated with founders Earl Clark, Harold Jones, Bernard Grobus, Willliam Scheider, and Ken Lindal for a suitable site and facility to meet community needs. (Courtesy Upper Mountain Fire Company.)

The first Lewiston town meeting was held at the house of Sparrow Sage on Ridge Road near Model City Road not far from the site of the current town hall. Justices of the Peace Rufus Spaulding and Gideon Frisbee called the meeting to order, which divided the town into 11 road districts. In 1972, the town debated the issue of sharing facilities with the village. L. C. Williams photographed the interior of the town hall in 1973. (Courtesy *Niagara Gazette*.)

CHAPTER 6

ARTPARK, ENTERTAINMENT, AND EATERIES

By the Lower Landing of the portage and the gateway to the west, state senate majority leader Earl Brydges proclaimed at the groundbreaking ceremonies for the Niagara Frontier Performing Arts Center on May 14, 1970, "Audiences will enjoy the great sounds of symphonies, the grace of ballet, and the excitement of historical pageants." (Courtesy Buffalo State College Courier-Express Collection.)

The Art-El, a partially enclosed L-shaped boardwalk built shortly after the theater opened and photographed by the Simonsons, was the heart of the activity of the visual arts and shelter for artists' work. The artists-in-residence worked at the park for one to 10 weeks. Art-El was razed several years ago. In 2009, concertgoers approached the security checkpoint for the free Tuesday in the Park or Wednesdays on the Gorge summer concerts. (Courtesy of the Historical Association of Lewiston.)

ARTPARK, ENTERTAINMENT, AND EATERIES

The 2,400-seat Artpark theater, in this *Niagara Gazette* photograph, was built by the New York State Commission of Parks and Recreation and funded by the Natural Heritage Trust. The 1974 gala performance opened with the Buffalo Philharmonic Orchestra, Canadian contralto Maureen Forrester, conductor Michael Tilson Thomas, actress Cicely Tyson, and dancer Edward Villella. Dignitaries and patrons enjoyed Tchaikovsky's *1812 Overture*, champagne, and fireworks. One of the 2009 stage spectaculars was *Joseph and the Amazing Technicolor Dreamcoat*. (Courtesy of the Historical Association of Lewiston.)

The stone columns supported the cables of the Lewiston-Queenston Suspension Bridge in this 1938 photograph. The last cables of the early bridge were removed in 1962. The 35-ton steel structure, the *Omega*, created by artist Owen Morrel, opened in the summer of 1980 as an observation deck. The artwork closed in recent years due to safety concerns. Hikers can walk from here to sections of the Gorge Trail. (Courtesy Buffalo State College Courier-Express Collection.)

ARTPARK, ENTERTAINMENT, AND EATERIES

James Cleghorn built the stone mansion at the south end of Niagara Street in 1834. Pictured in this 1941 image, the residence of generations of Scovells was known as Oak Hill. The building was destroyed by fire in 1964. Part of the garden walls and the stone foundation are still visible. The Hopewellian-style burial mound, dated AD 160+-80 by radiocarbon testing, north of the stone ruins is the most sacred area at Artpark. (Courtesy of Historical Association of Lewiston.)

Artpark patrons and residents enjoy a variety of food services in the village. John Kudla photographed Lewiston's shortest St. Patrick's Day parade, the length of the Buena Vista Restaurant (year unknown). Buena Vista Restaurant patrons in 1955 enjoyed mambo night and dance instruction by Fred Jones of the Havana Club. Gene and Helen Parrone operated the Buena Vista and Lewiston Sunoco. In 2008, the English-style Lewiston Village Pub opened with 20 beer taps and serves pub fare. (Courtesy *Niagara Gazette*.)

ARTPARK, ENTERTAINMENT, AND EATERIES

Jacob Townsend resided here around 1818. Townsend, Bronson, and Company built ships used during the War of 1812. Andrew Susty photographed the 1980 Clarkson House opened by Robert and Marilyn Clarkson as a steak and lobster house in 1958. Macri's Italian Grille and Catering opened September 8, 2009, changing the half-century-old name of this restaurant. Casa Antica Ristorante, also a family-run restaurant on Center Street, specializes in both southern and northern Italian cuisine. (Courtesy of the Historical Association of Lewiston.)

Bjarne Klaussen, the former Hooker Electrochemical Company president, resided at 703 Center Street for 27 years. In 1967, a proposed gas station on the site prompted historic-minded citizenry to garner the attention of Gov. Nelson Rockefeller and Lady Bird Johnson to save this structure built in 1820 by Dr. Willard Smith. Michael Broderick and Robin Faulring opened the Orange Cat Coffee Company in July 2004. Coffees and organic teas delight patrons and Tuesday Artpark performers. (Courtesy of the Historical Association of Lewiston.)

Artpark, Entertainment, and Eateries

Eddie Marchitelli established the Paint Shop in 1964 and changed the name to Eddie's Art Shoppe with the addition of picture framing. Bob Darin took over in 1982 and moved to Grand Island in 2009. To the left in this mid-1960s photograph is Charlie Corieri's Lewiston Restaurant that Charlie ran until his retirement in 1972. Presently from the left to right are the China House (out of view), the Steelhead Irish Pub and Restaurant, Mary Josephine Boutique, and Village Antiques. (Courtesy Eddie's Art Shoppe.)

Pictured left, out of view, the popular eatery Apple Granny's Restaurant opened in 1975 in Helms' Grocery Store. Gordon Harper managed the Coat of Arms restaurant, named by contest winner Norma Dixon in 1967. Harry Mooradian took over from 1971 until 1980. Currently Carmelo's Restaurant, run by chef Carmelo Raimondi (following his father), continues to offer fine American and continental cuisine of local foods. On the right are Allstate Insurance, Bee Hive, and the Village Bake Shoppe. (Courtesy of the Historical Association of Lewiston.)

ARTPARK, ENTERTAINMENT, AND EATERIES

Schneider's, the first licensed Lewiston restaurant after Prohibition, suffered a fire in 1972 as photographed by the *Niagara Gazette*. In March 2004, owners Eric Matthews and Ken Bryan, partners since 1994 operating the Tin Pan Alley on Cayuga Street, opened the popular Brickyard Pub and BBQ. Manager Steve Matthews suggested a smokehouse after extensive remodeling of the restaurant and removing four ceiling layers. Next door, the Brio Pizzeria and Restaurant serves gourmet pizza. (Courtesy of the Historical Association of Lewiston.)

The luxury Barton Hill Hotel and Spa replaced the residential area on First Street at Center Street. The hotel, owned by Edward and Diane Finkbeiner, opened in 2007 as "life as it was meant to be lived." During the summer of 2009, the hotel graciously hosted a rain location for Jazz at the Gazebo and the Historical Association of Lewiston's monthly meetings. Southwest of Barton Hill is Water Street Landing, built in 1871, offering popular Frank Sinatra–style music on Tuesdays. (Courtesy *Niagara Gazette*.)

ARTPARK, ENTERTAINMENT, AND EATERIES

The Silo, a coal storage elevator, was the last trace of the prosperous shipping port in Lewiston. The Niagara Navigation Company began operations in 1878, carrying passengers and freight. Thousands of tourists disembarked from the Great Lakes steamers that ran between Toronto and Lewiston. The Cibola steamer caught fire at the dock, which spread to the American Hotel that was rebuilt as the Cornell House. In 1998, Richard Hastings opened the popular Silo Restaurant. (Courtesy of the Historical Association of Lewiston.)

From left to right are Eva Nicklas, Ernie Murdoch, Julio Coangelo, and James Rhoney. They donated paint, money, and man power to paint the Hennepin Park Gazebo at Fourth and Center Streets around 1992 for the growing number of events sponsored by Lewiston Council on the Arts. Blue Mondays at the Gazebo received the *Blues Beat Magazine's* prestigious Muddy Award for 16 years of great music. World-class musicians performed at Lewiston's eighth-annual jazz festival in 2009. (Courtesy of the Historical Association of Lewiston.)

ARTPARK, ENTERTAINMENT, AND EATERIES

CHAPTER

7

TRANSFORMATION
AND STREETSCAPES

The village has experienced a significant transformation since the 1970s era Power Authority photograph showing the Silo at bottom left, south of the Riverside Inn (now Water Street Landing). The streetscape project completed in 2001 enhanced the efforts to develop Lewiston into a major Western New York destination during the summer festival season. (Courtesy of the Niagara Falls Library Local History Department.)

77

Brothers Alphonse and Leonard DiMino opened TOPS Friendly Market in 1964, advertising "The supermarket with old-fashioned ideas. We have people. You don't have to talk to yourself." Mary Rose Casero said, "My father Alphonse was a great guy. He always thought of others." In 1998, the first building was razed and a time capsule was placed in the pillars with the old crossed ties that employees wore with white shirts from the first store. (Courtesy Anthony DiMino.)

Lewiston businessman Emery Simon purchased the Ford Veterinary Center property in 2000. The house was placed on the giant remote controlled roller ready for the short trek across the street to the corner of Center and Ninth Streets. The journey of the historic Piper's Law Office, known as the "Little Blue House," to Academy Park finally happened November 19, 2009. The structure is to be remodeled for a new tourist welcome center by the village. (Courtesy *Niagara Gazette*.)

The parking lot at Center Street and Portage Road once held the dormitory for the academy. The Kodak Film Fotomat building was recently remodeled and became Jane's Cafe Express in the parking lot of Natural Link and Hibbard's Custard Stand. South on Portage Road, Syros Greek and American Restaurant opened in September 2008 in Clark's Burgerhouse that closed in 2007 after being rebuilt in 2004. The popular breakfast and lunch operation burned in 2001. (Courtesy of the Niagara Falls Library Local History Department.)

Jason Marshall, D.D.S., converted the former Buena Vista apartments to Lewiston Family Dental, which opened in July 2005. Samuel Bruni, William Brown, William Moody, and Frederick Niland practiced dentistry in 1957 in the village. Niland was the inspiration for the World War II movie *Saving Private Ryan*. Also in the 1950s, medical doctors Henry Alderman (700 Center Street) and Hans Selzer (500 Center Street) treated patients, and Coulson's Pharmacy (486 Center Street) and Stine's Drug Store (417 Center Street) filled prescriptions. (Courtesy of William Scully.)

Vincenzo's Pizza, open for more than 30 years at 742 Center Street, has been surrounded by changes. At left out of view, the Opera House was the town supervisor's office in the early 1970s. Today Organic Health and Beauty Center, law offices, and Lewiston Council on the Arts activities are at the Opera House. Michael's Electric Appliance sold goods in 1959, and now, 50 years later, it is Angel to Apple. Sue's Frame of Mind opened in December 2009. (Courtesy of the Historical Association of Lewiston.)

TRANSFORMATION AND STREETSCAPES

The 1820 Bates Cook law office at 755 Center Street was Sam Russo's art studio when Emery Simon purchased the property in 1989. The Dent Foundation and the Brockden Group, an advertising agency, are tenants. The house on the right was removed to make way for the plaza that became the new office for the Marine Trust Company in 1958. The sign for 755 advertises the tenants of the two modern buildings in the rear. (Courtesy of the Historical Association of Lewiston.)

In this 1972 photograph, from left to right are Quote and Quill, Village Vendor, Robert Beck's stained-glass shop, and Francis Optical operated on Center Street. Bobby Scully, owner of the Village Vendor, always promoted Lewiston. During the 1950s and 1960s, the Clay Pipe, Lewiston Decorating Service, Cary Insurance, and McBride's Shoes operated in these shops. Today Gourmet Food and Gifts, Village Vineyard Wine Shop, Mode Image Cosmetics Salon, and Ashker's Juice Bar serve the community. (Courtesy of the Historical Association of Lewiston.)

TRANSFORMATION AND STREETSCAPES

Public Library, Lewiston. N. Y.

Charles Hotchkiss managed a general store here, built around the 1820s by his brother, Calvin. The Lewiston Library, in this early 1900s postcard, was located in this building from 1908 to 1961. Tomaso and Addolorata Di Camillo opened their first bakery in Niagara Falls in 1920. The family delivered bread in horse-drawn wagons. The Di Camillos opened their Lewiston bakery in 1980 in the old library building; this bakery is one of five retail outlets owned by the family. Di Camillo baked goods can be found all over the world. (Courtesy of William Scully.)

TRANSFORMATION AND STREETSCAPES

The 1838 Hotchkiss building housed Vevirit Hardware, managed by Joseph Vevirit from 1950 to 1953. Lawrence Jensen, a commander of Lewiston Post 1083 American Legion, then sold hardware here for 15 years. Sleds for the 1963 Christmas season sold for $4.50 and hockey sticks for $1. For a short time, a ceramics shop and the Village Pottery preceded Kivi Realty. Hunt Realty, of three Hunt family generations since 1911, conducts business now at 479 Center Street. (Courtesy *Niagara Gazette*.)

TRANSFORMATION AND STREETSCAPES

J. Boardman Scovell practiced law in the *c.* 1858 Scovell building. In the 1940s, Hap Brown recalled hearing Scovell thank Orville Wright for a Paris postage stamp. For his birthday present, Scovell went to London with his grandmother in 1887 for the Golden Jubilee celebration of Queen Victoria. Dominic Notarianni of Francesco's Hair Fashions added the east building in 1977. Tenants are Derivier Jewelers, Lewiston Chiropractic, McKay Massage Therapy, and Jude Violante, D.P.M. (Courtesy of the Historical Association of Lewiston.)

Philbrick's Gas Station at 424 Center Street charged "old-time prices 32.9¢ and 34.9¢" in 1972. The late 1950s service stations on Center Street were Boyd's, Cooper's Esso, Hick's Esso, Herbert Nickerson's, Marshall's, Vincent and Son, and Wright's Esso. Perkins Oil on Portage Road and McKay Oil at First and Tuscarora Streets sold home fuel oil. Marcella's Hair Studio and Michelle Baker's shop, Luxuries for Less, opened in September 2008 and operate in the renovated building. (Courtesy of the Historical Association of Lewiston.)

Lewiston Fire Company No. 1 formed in 1914 as a bucket brigade. Each member kept two buckets to respond to the Presbyterian church bell. A fire hall with a siren on top was erected at 444–446 Center Street in 1927. Standing in front of the fire hall around 1936, from left to right are Victor VanDenBosch, Seymour Krohn, Phil McCabe, Sydney Smith, Emerson Walker, Red Fleming, and Theodore Helpap. The former storage building for Edwin Mellen Press is for sale. (Courtesy Elizabeth Jordan.)

Kilmer's Esso Service Center ran the station in 1972 known as Hick's Esso in the late 1950s and 1960s. The old gas station purchased by Herbert Richardson sat vacant for a number of years. Additions and expansion at the corner of Fourth and Center Streets showcase the opportunities for the growing number of shops and artistic flavor of the heart of the village. Brick sidewalks, coach lights, and hanging flower baskets also enhance the street. (Courtesy of the Historical Association of Lewiston.)

TRANSFORMATION AND STREETSCAPES

The Bun Jo Motel owned by John Vrooman moved from Bridge Street near the foot of the Lewiston Suspension Bridge to South Water Street during the construction of Artpark. Since 1989, owners Bruce and Andrea Blakelock manage the motel known as the Riverside Sportsfishing and Motel. Captain Blakelock's fishing guide service provides year-round charters in the Niagara River and Lake Ontario, advertised as "one of the top Salmon and Steelhead Trout fishing spots in the world." (Courtesy of William Scully.)

The Niagara Frontier Bible Church purchased the former seminary of the Oblates of St. Francis de Sales in 1979. Eleanor Larson photographed the congregation as they prepared to move in 2003. Waste Technology Services (WTS) remodeled the 1848 residence and changed the 20th-century religious character and stained-glass windows. "WTS develops and implements by-product management systems for large industries with a focus on reuse/recycle opportunities for cost savings, operational efficiencies, and environmental compliance." (Courtesy Niagara Frontier Bible Church.)

Ron Schifferle photographed the 1990 construction of the Lewiston Public Library at 305 South Eighth Street. When the new library building was dedicated in 1991, former U.S. presidents Ford, Carter, Nixon, and Reagan sent autographed copies of their books. A local history and genealogy room and a children's wing were added in 1999. The Lewiston Public Library began in 1901 when the Men's Club of Lewiston held a New Year's party and each member donated two books. (Courtesy *Niagara Gazette*.)

Lewiston has a long tradition of community service. Pictured is the food tent at the 1960 Peach Festival, sponsored by the Kiwanis Club of Lewiston. From left to right cooking burgers and hot dogs are Bob Lowe, Tom Beachy, and Devillo "Sam" Gray. The Kiwanis Club of Lewiston was chartered on May 17, 1958, with 64 members. The hamburger flippers at the September 2009 Peach Festival from left to right are Jerry Wolfgang, "Bud" Griffith, Tom Beachy, Ed Evert, and Tom Minarcin. (Courtesy Terry Collesano.)

The Freedom Crossing Monument landmark was unveiled on October 14, 2009, at the Lewiston Landing Park. Lezlie Harper Wells, a "descendent of freedom seekers" who crossed the Niagara River, participated in the unveiling program. The monument portrays Josiah Tryon, the Underground Railroad stationmaster, helping escaped slaves into his rowboat on the bank of the Niagara River headed to Canada. Susan Geissler, one of America's premier sculptors, designed and created this dramatic landmark. (Both, courtesy photographer Amy Lynn Freiermuth.)

www.arcadiapublishing.com

Discover books about the town where you grew up, the cities where your friends and families live, the town where your parents met, or even that retirement spot you've been dreaming about. Our Web site provides history lovers with exclusive deals, advanced notification about new titles, e-mail alerts of author events, and much more.

Find Your Place in History.